Psychic Medium: Channelling, Clairvoyance, & Spiritual Communication For "Healing" and Light Work

not engaging in the rendering of legal, financial, medical or professional advice.

By reading this document, the reader agrees that under no circumstances are we responsible for any losses, direct or indirect, which are incurred as a result of the use of information contained within this document, including, but not limited to, —errors, omissions, or inaccuracies.

Table of Contents

Introduction

Are you fascinated with anything related to spirits, immaterial entities, and angels? Then learning more about mediumship and its branches is something that you ought to do. Mediumship refers to a person's ability, someone who acts as the medium or channel, to experience communicating with the spirits of those who have already passed away, as well as other immaterial entities including angels.

If you plan to become a medium, then your goal is to facilitate the process of establishing a connection with spirits who wish to relay messages to non-mediums. Mediumship also requires a medium to sense spirits, those who are part of this world before but have already departed. Note, however, that this goal is not limited to that. Mediums can also connect to and sense angels and spirit guides, interpret their messages and relay them to the living.

While this is not an easy thing to do, everyone is actually capable of honing their mediumship or psychic abilities. There are those who naturally have this ability while others still need to sharpen this skill. If you are still at the stage of familiarizing yourself about everything related to mediumship, then this book is for you. It contains relevant information about mediumship, what you need to become a medium, benefits of honing your psychic or mediumship abilities, how to decipher the messages of those who are no longer on the Earth and how to further improve your skill.

With this book, you will become one of the best mediums this world will ever have. You will be on your way toward enjoying the fascinating journey of spiritual opening and awakening with the help of the contents of this book.

Chapter 1 – An Overview of Mediumship

Mediumship and psychic ability is actually a gift. It is not a curse as some others might view it. However, it is only you who is capable of seeing the entire practice as a real gift, instead of a curse. If you are still a beginner, or someone who is actually afraid of spirits and the dead in the first place, you may start to ask questions like "Why would anyone want to become a medium?" or "Is it right to pursue honing your psychic and mediumship abilities?" You may also start seeking for validation to determine if you picked the right life path once you start to gain interest in mediumship.

While mediumship can be fun to learn about, there is a lot of seriousness and responsibilities added to it. The true essence of mediumship lies in putting all your energy into going into a world which is beyond one's imagination. Spiritualists follow two kinds of psychic readings – mental and physical mediumships.

We are going to focus on psychic readers that follow mental mediumships. In this form of mediumship, the psychic reader can feel, listen and see spirits and symbols in their mind's eye. For this, it is very important for the reader to be mentally and emotionally healthy. A quality psychic reader is a channel between a person and their loved ones in the form of spirits; a good medium will always be truthful towards his or her clients and will never misuse their ability to connect with spirits.

This is the main reason why the first step in becoming a medium is to accept that you have such an ability, that you are interested in this field, and that you have what it takes to relay the messages of the spirits to the living. Once you accept that fact, you can easily embrace the path that you are about to take. You can also start embracing the fact that becoming a medium is actually beneficial. Here are just some of the many positive things that you will enjoy once you become a medium:

You can connect with angels, your loved ones, and personal guides

Mediumship does not only involve connecting with spirits for others to receive and send messages to their angels and loved ones. It is also good for you because you can connect with spirits in case you need to do so for personal reasons. One of the greatest things about honing this ability is that you can instantly access the spiritual realm, regardless of who you want to connect to and your reasons for doing so. Learning this art for your benefit is good as long as it does not harm anyone else or it is not learned to put someone else into trouble. Practicing mediumship can help you strengthen your personal intuition which can help you regardless of whether you are in your psychic mode or not.

You have easy access to a support team all the time

Opening your skill to communicate with spirits and those who are not part of this world may either exhilarate or frighten you at first, but eventually, you will calm down and enjoy the fact that the spirits who surround you are not actually there to scare or frighten you. They are there to be your friends, instead. This is a good thing because you can receive divine support and guidance anytime you need it.

You can ask your loved ones, angels and your own guides to give you certain answers and solutions to whatever challenges that you are currently facing. You will feel like you have friends who can offer you the support that you need, and the catch – they are usually available to offer their help anytime. They will be there to explain everything to you in a more comprehensive and cohesive manner. You will never feel alone.

You will experience spiritual transformation, which promotes self-healing

Aside from delivering messages to other people, the spirits with whom you connect also have potent messages that they wish to deliver to you. Some spirits, guides, and angels are sneaky enough that they will do everything to improve your skill to connect with them. In most cases, this will also result in enlightening other areas of your life that you need to examine, which is good for self-healing.

Working with spirits allows you to gain some soulful realizations, and these can actually let you change for the better. You will most likely learn about forgiveness and love, and about the specific things that hold you back. You will also know exactly how you can release negativities. The reason is that the spirits readily talk about such things – those they regretted, wish they'd done when they were still alive, and the things they are supposed to do in case they get the chance to live again.

Being a medium, you listen to the messages that they transmit, so there is a great chance that you will learn valuable lessons from them. This makes it easier for you to heal, change and explore some vital areas of your life that you have actually overlooked before.

The ability to connect with positive and quality spirits can help you expand your emotional and mental dimension and not only that, you can also liberate others through the extensive knowledge you gain from the experiences of spirits. You develop the potential to stay calm and composed in whichever situation you are in, and it saves you from making any kind of decision that you would later regret. It serves as your personal guide for emancipation from all unhealthy inclinations and eccentricities.

You will no longer fear death

Starting to communicate with spirits can make you realize how active, aware and alive they are. They are still fully aware of the life here on Earth even when they have already departed. You will gather information from them about how they managed to still get involved in the lives of their loved ones, closest friends and families even if they are no longer with them physically.

You will know some of the things that they try to do to extend their help to their living loved ones, although they are already spirits. This can help change your perception of death. You will realize that even after death, there is still life. Your spirit will still be alive in essence. The only difference is that you will not have a dense physical body. Communicating with spirits regularly is actually an eye-opener.

It can be really scary to deal with spirits initially, especially when you are in your learning stage. When we talk about spirits we always have a negative image about them, and we always speak about the adversities they bring into a person's life but when you get accustomed to talking to people who are not alive you realize the importance of life. Through spirits and supernatural energies, you get to know how essential moments are while you are alive and what is it that you can do to improve your lifestyle as a whole.

You get the chance to connect with your deceased loved ones

If you already have deceased loved ones, then your mediumship ability gives you the chance to connect with them, as well. You can do this without the need for another medium. You can easily reunite with the spirits of your beloved departed.

Connecting with the ones you have loved the most during their lifespan can be really encouraging. We all feel the most motivated by the ones we are connected to the most. Imagine being in touch with your deceased loved one who understood you the most and was a confidant when they were alive. If you are someone who likes being alone in her or himself or if you find it difficult to connect with people re-establishing a connection with your beloved can help you release your emotional baggage and can bring peace to you.

You can start manifesting things in a quicker manner

You can collaborate with your angels and spirit guides to manifest the things that you desire much quicker into your life. This is one of the benefits of being a spiritual communicator. Since you can easily access guidance from spirits, staying on track with the purpose of your own soul and aligning all aspects of your life with who you really are is easier. This makes it easier for you to accomplish all your goals.

The best thing is that good souls will always inspire you to lead a life that is simple, positive and goal-oriented. You can seek the assistance of spirits to keep you motivated when you feel things are not working as you've planned; it happens to all of us. We all need support to stay focused and motivated to fulfill your desires in our lives. It gets easier to follow your dreams when you have a positive inspiration and force guiding you through all your good and bad times and to keep you rooted.

Being a channeler or medium can seem strange but believe it or not it is one step you can take towards transforming yourself into a constructive and more productive being which will help in your growth and development. It doesn't end here; you will also experience a version of you that is upbeat, peaceful and confident – a side of you that will work for you. Being a medium is the greatest gift you can give yourself and humankind because this is one of the most effective ways you can bring happiness and light to the lives of people who are searching for unanswered questions.

Chapter 2 – Types of Mediumship

Psychic ability comes in different types. If you are interested in undergoing psychic development, you have to learn about each type, so you can choose which exactly among the different types work for you. While some types are common, there are also others that are extremely rare, yet really fascinating. Some types are capable of giving you an unforgettable out of body experience while others can provide you with a form of healing, which works from the inside out.

This chapter is designed to explain to you some of the most common types of mediumship, so you will become more familiar with each one.

Physical mediumship

This type of mediumship works by creating a physical phenomenon. These usually cover things like creating ectoplasm via the visiting spirit, smoke billet pictures, tipping of tables and noise making levitation. If you plan to become a physical medium, then be prepared to work together with the spirit to produce a physical phenomenon. The phenomenon is something that all those who are around can also experience using at least one of their physical senses.

Physical mediumship is the highest form of evidence where you see spirits taking over a live body to come into its actualization. This medium being a physical one needs you to put your body through pain which could leave you hurting or sick for a while – a few hours or a few days. You may also feel a little tired due to the process this transition follows. In the process where you try to bring a deceased loved one into actualization where it takes the form of the body that they were in when they were alive, you could experience your body forming into the kind that they had, which means if they had any physical issues, scars or any similar marks, these may manifest themselves on or within your body. Physical mediumship is done in the dark with low lights dimmed in the colors blue and red. This form of mediumship is a distinctive and one of a kind gift.

Some examples of physical mediumship include the following:

- **Materialization** – Here, the spirits utilize ectoplasm as a means of clothing themselves, making their physical appearance even more apparent to everyone who is present. The spirit that comes into a medium's body can transform into the way they looked when they were alive whether it is their clothing or physical features. Materialized spirits are often seen as dancing, communicating or even showcasing gestures such as embracing, kissing, holding hands or similar ones. It is also seen in some cases where spirits pass through walls and/or dematerialize in from of the onlookers.

- **Transfiguration** – This happens when the spirit makes a mask of ectoplasm, then places this in front of your face. It is in this mask where the spirit's face will appear, allowing him to talk directly to someone, especially his loved one. If your loved ones had any marks or features like a beard or mustache, it could be evidently seen on the medium's face bringing a total change overall. You may also see a change in the size and formation of the body of the medium which can be really fascinating, an illusion that can boggle one's mind.

- **Independent and direct voice** – In the direct voice phenomenon, voice trumpets are utilized, and these serve as condensers for the voices of the spirits. You also need to attach a voice box into the trumpet. This is where the spirits will speak through. Independent voice, on the other hand, takes place when the spirit speaks in any part of the room even without using a trumpet.

- **Percussion** – This happens when the spirit produces sound by rattling tambourines, ringing bells or knocking on walls.

- **Levitation** – This physical phenomenon is characterized by lifting objects or people with the help of ectoplasmic rods.

- **Telekinesis** – This is characterized by the movement of objects, which is possible through mind power. In some cases, the spirit does not need to intervene.

- **Spirit lights/Light work** – This happens when everyone in the room where the physical mediumship session is taking place witnesses the dancing colored lights brought on by the spirits.

These are just some examples of how physical mediumship takes place. Those who are in the spiritual world always work together, so they can produce more phenomena designed to help physical mediums overcome the difficulties in connecting to those on the other side. When physical mediumship takes place, you can expect everyone who is around to witness the entire process. It is physical and real. Note, however, that this form is the rarest among the different types of mediumship.

Mediumship in the form of a physical psychic is a very lengthy process. It takes a great amount of concentration and dedication to reach a level where you can bring together two energies which are the spirit and your own energy. People in modern times have taken a step back in performing such an activity due to the time and effort needed to see and feel noticeable happenings and vibrations.

Mental mediumship

This form of mediumship involves relying on mental processes or the mind to establish effective spiritual communication. A mental medium is capable of hearing or seeing communication from the other side. He can then share what he hears or sees to the right people. If you aim to practice mental mediumship, then note that you have the freedom to choose which messages you should share and which you should not share.

It is because it is you who is fully aware of the whole process. You can develop the skills of a good mental medium in just a short span of time. You can even learn the skills within just a few weeks, provided you are guided by a good teacher and the right training materials.

The best utilization of mental mediumship can bring in a lot of change in the lives of psychic readers personally. Imagine developing a skill where you practice concentration and connect with high-quality spirits that in turn help you bring out a superlative side of you. One thing you must take care of is that you must use it to bring positivity rather than attempting to put down someone or harming someone negatively. This is a very powerful source of energy to be used to add value to your existence.

Mental mediumship is angelic and has to be done in the best interest of yourself and the people who seek your help. Serving people who want to create a connection with their dear ones beyond the limits of life can bring peace of mind which will bring peace and happiness to your life.

Mental mediumship is also further classified into the following forms:

- **Clairvoyance** – Clairvoyance in general terms means second sight. This type of mental mediumship allows you to witness spirit personalities. There are even times when you see the spirits as if they are real, moving in a more natural and normal way. What makes clairvoyance different from other forms of mental mediumship is that it is only the medium who witnesses the spirits. Others who are present in the session are incapable of seeing them. As the medium, you are given the chance to pass on to others what you see through evidence.

  Also, in clairvoyance, the spiritual communication process works with the help of images. It could be an image from your mind's eye, or in some cases, you may actually witness an object or a spirit as if it is actually looking at you in the eye. If you practice this form of mental mediumship, expect to see not only the spirit but also a symbol, scene or object. In case you see the actual person who conveys the message or information, expect this message to be more direct and straightforward. The problem, however, is how you will describe what you saw to those who are present.

When we speak about clairvoyance and visualizing things through this technique, you must be careful when you choose your words in the form of a question to which you want an answer or statement which you want to happen. For instance, you may wish to find a handsome looking man or a beautiful looking woman for a dance night – *'Will I get a chance to dance with a good looking partner at the dance party tonight?'* You can find as many answers as you want if you believe in this approach. Framing a sentence plays a vital role so choose your words wisely.

- **Clairaudience** – In this form, the spiritual medium is capable of hearing sounds including voices, and this is where the process of communicating with the spirits takes place. In general terms, clairaudience is an approach where you can hear voices or sounds that are not audible to most other people. Just like in clairvoyance, you may also hear the sounds either through your mind or through your physical ear when you are practicing clairaudience. The problem is that when other sounds, like music, take place, you may have a hard time deciphering and interpreting the correct message. This is the main reason why just like in clairvoyance, you need to really hone your skill in this area.

As the medium, you are the only one who can hear the message, and you can pass on the message of the spirit based on what you want to share. The message is capable of providing comfort to a bereaved relative, loved one or friend.

To come across such voices, you need to be in a quiet area or at a place where there is extreme silence. It is easy to know if you are a clairaudient – yes, it is! You could be someone who listens to voices or who has an ability to listen to sounds that are unknown to others. So how do you find out? People who possess this skill are usually sensitive towards loud noises, they often talk to themselves, their close ones are imaginary, and music makes them connect to their souls.

An important fact about clairaudience is that you may hear voices that are unusual and could be scary because it is connected to spirits from the outer world. The best ways to develop your skills of clairaudience is to listen carefully, practice and imagine, listen to classical music and meditate.

- **Clairsentience** – In this form of mental mediumship, you, as the psychic medium, are capable of sensing the presence of spirits. You can also sense the words that they say. You will get a feel of the presence of spirits once you sense their actual presence and emotions. You can also sense them through changes in temperatures, smell, fragrance or scent, breezes or a certain feeling where there seems to be cobwebs on your face. Note, however, that there are times when these sensations and impressions are vague, making the whole process harder to decipher.

Clairsentience in general terms means clear sensing. It relates to feeling the present, past and future emotional and physical states of others using senses which are other than the normal ones. The psychics who have an ability to gauge information from areas such as houses and buildings are the ones who possess clairsentience skills. This form of mediumship is where you follow your instincts, guts or insights. You may feel more sympathetic and / or empathetic of people too much – such people may have major emotional issues that could be unhealthy. Sensations that occur in your body at places or points also come under this form. Some people may experience touch in terms of pulling, nudging or tapping. People who are deeply attached to someone emotionally can feel their presence under this form; you may sense that the person you are attached to is close and is watching you.

These forms of mediumship are unusual and may not be found in many people. No doubt you can develop the ability to feel these feelings by focusing and meditation. The most important thing is that you must be strong enough to take in such sensations. It could be really scary if you are not mentally prepared to get reactions from spirits in any shape, arrangement or frame.

Trance mediumship

In trance mediumship, the blending of energies between the medium and the spirit communicator takes place. The blending process actually varies in intensity and degree. While the spiritual communicator does not need to get into the physical state of the medium, he tends to work with the help of the medium's aura. Note, however, that whatever the spirit does is with the medium's permission, so there is no such thing as the spirit taking over the mind and body of the medium in this form.

When the medium is in a deep trance, with his permission, of course, he may start showing a different personality. He will start to talk directly to someone while also displaying different gestures, mannerisms, tone of voice, age, accent, and gender. The situation is so different that those who witness it firsthand may think that it is no longer right. If you are a medium, then note that you can withdraw and disengage from your own self, giving the spirit the chance to function using your consciousness.

It should be noted, however, that in case you are in an extremely deep trance, you will not have conscious awareness of the communication's content. To ensure the accuracy of the message and keep the communication process free flowing, some mediumship experts suggest that the medium should put their preconceptions and ego aside. The medium should also be non-attached when it comes to the content of the message. The participants also need to maintain their discernment and objectivity to ensure that the message is clearly deciphered.

Trance mediumship, also known as channeling, is a form where you need extreme focus. This medium allows minds to convey thoughts by putting aside ego barriers. Also, you must know sleepwalking is not a part of trance mediumship as they are two different occurrences.

These are the cardinal mediumships that spirits actualize in. These forms of psychics are very interesting and can be very beneficial to humankind. There has been a clear decrease of physical mediumship in modern times due to the amount of focus and work it needs, whereas mental mediumship has gained popularity in today's age as it brings in positivity and encouragement in a medium. Personally, the medium will feel a transition from leading a good or bad to a better life, and if taken up professionally they can help other people reconnect with their loved ones, which brings great mental satisfaction.

Chapter 3 – Some Myths about Mediumship

Mediumship is one of the most controversial and confusing subjects that has ever graced the Earth. Many believe in the validity of the process while others don't totally believe that there is such thing as communicating with spirits. If you are one of those who is still at the stage of wondering what exactly mediums can do and can't do, then this chapter of this book will help you.

People have huge misconceptions about mediumship. A lot of people feel that mediumship or channeling has got something to do with special powers given by God, but that's not true. As humans, we all possess an ability to sense the power around us. No doubt this process takes effort and a lot of focus which is why not everybody can pursue psychic paths.

Here, some of the most common beliefs regarding mediumship will be explained, so you will know whether there is some truth to them:

Myth #1 – A great medium or psychic is capable of seeing the future

This is one of the biggest myths of all. Mediums and psychics have no way of seeing the future. They can't predict the next winning lottery numbers, or when someone can completely settle his mortgage or move to his dream destination. Future predictions are not a guaranteed skillset of mediums. What mediums and psychics do, actually, include obtaining information without any scientific knowledge. Most psychics who base their readings on intuition also give prospective outcomes of situations. They can't predict your future because the future can also change itself based on your choices and actions. There are possibilities where psychic readers can gauge upcoming events, but as it's mentioned, there are possibilities that circumstances may change.

Myth #2 – A certified medium is capable of providing better and more accurate psychic readings

Not true. The primary reason is that the mediumship industry is not actually regulated. Those who intend to work in this field don't need to finish a course or pass a board exam to practice and open up their own business. Mediums who claim that they are certified are actually those who simply spent money to attend some classes. The tests designed to obtain certificates are also often ungoverned and unregulated.

Those who use their intuition to practice are also capable, but there are times when this is not enough to guarantee one hundred percent accurate readings. If you are serious about finding a good medium, then a wise piece of advice is to find someone with many years of experience in the field and has a huge amount of positive feedback. This indicates that he or she has a high client satisfaction rate.

Psychic readings are based on the concentration and effort put in by the medium. A certificate could be an addition to the doings of a psychic reader but unless there is enough focus to connect with outer energies a medium cannot bring the best out of his or her practice.

Myth #3 – Mediums and psychics can read your mind

Mediums and psychics can't read exactly what is on your mind. Many people mistakenly believe that psychics and mediums are so adept in mind reading that they start asking them questions like "When is my birthday?" or "How many fingers am I currently hiding behind my back?" Most psychics say that they can't read exactly what is on their client's mind, or guess what they are thinking or what they are feeling. They just have the gift of empathy, which lets them pick up their clients' dominant feelings.

If one is upset, frustrated, angry, worried, depressed, or anxious, for instance, he can send a signal that a psychic or medium can energetically read. Once the signal is sent, the medium can then use clairaudience, clairvoyance or any other form of mediumship to know exactly why you feel or think that way. However, avoid asking him the exact thing that is on your mind since he has no means of accessing such info.

Psychics and mediums, however, are capable of accessing your spirit guides. Most of them do their psychic and mind readings with the help of spirit guides. These guides can tell them many things. For instance, your spirit guide can tell a medium about your current job, your dream job, how you can make the transition and whether or not you are currently in an abusive relationship.

A psychic reader has the ability to comfort their client and gauge positive and negative energies around them but getting into a person's thoughts can be difficult. Mediums are the ones who can connect you with your loved ones and help you get information that you need depending on how the spirits respond to them.

Myth #4 – Getting a psychic reading from a medium will cause spirits to start following you around

Not true. Note that spirits are already around you even if you haven't received readings before. However, you'll become more sensitive to their presence once you undergo a mediumship or psychic session because this can shift your awareness of them. You will become more sensitive to the process of spiritual communication.

Perhaps you didn't mind too much when you heard sounds late at night before, but when you received a psychic reading, you suddenly think of spirits as possible reasons for such noises. Shifting your awareness regarding the presence of the spirits can also make you more open and accepting of them.

The spirits don't start following you after obtaining a reading. They are already around, and you have just become more sensitive to them.

These are just a few of the myths surrounding mediumship. Now that some truths about the process are revealed, you can readily accept what mediums and psychics can actually do.

You must understand there are unknown forces around you at all times, be it morning or afternoon or night. These energies are not felt by everyone as not all build on their ability to feel spirits around them. Most of us do not know how to build our abilities about understanding how this process works. But, the bottom line is there will be no adverse effects of going through a psychic reading to find your answers.

Myth #5 – Psychic readers are gifted by the Almighty above

Everybody possesses an ability to be a medium, and these mediums are not specially chosen. People feel psychic readers are gifted by God or spirits above. No, in fact, every one of us possesses the skill of being a medium. Most people do not know that the gift of being a medium is imbibed in one and all; some people choose to be a medium and develop their skill to help people and earn a living.

Let me give you a simple example. We all have intuitions – some of us follow them, some of us don't, again that is a choice and a gift given equally to all humankind by God. The people who develop their psyche could be someone among your group or someone you meet at a social gathering or parks and gardens or someone you may not have thought could be a medium. These are normal people!

Just as we have priests, actors, athletes, musicians and similar other artists who build their finesse, mediums are the ones who choose to evolve as powerful connectors and communicators. Psychic readers are purely human and work incredibly hard in building their skills so they can help themselves and the people who come to them to re-establish a connection with their loved ones and find answers to their questions.

Myth #6 – If a medium cannot connect to a spirit, something unfortunate is going to happen

There can be a lot of reasons why a medium might not connect with a spirit – it could just be bad timing, or it may not be the right day. This has nothing to do with evil happenings, and it is definitely not a dark or unknown secret. People misunderstand that not connecting with spirits means something negative will happen. You must know a good and learned medium will always put across to you positive energy and messages from the world of spirits. The world of spirits are supportive of you and would not harm you because if you thought they could, they would've done it already because they are around you all the time.

The fact is that sometimes you just don't feel right about getting a reading or appointment done, and that feeling is called intuition. That has got nothing to do with any mishaps so you can be carefree of the old tales you've heard from your grandma. Remember, your loved ones in the form of spirits have nothing to share but love and wish to bring harmony in your life. Think of it like this, if someone really loves you or you love someone with all your heart would he or she ever hurt you? Of course not! Your loved one, regardless of whether they have expired or are living with you, would never think of hurting you for the sake of their love.

Myth #7 – Mediumship is not a Profession – So why does a Psychic Reader take an emolument?

Mediumship is not a mere job you do from 9:00 AM to 7:00 PM with a set of protocols and syntax, but it is a consistent progression of strongly connecting with your loved ones. This is not an easy task, and it takes time and a lot of energy to engage with spirits in a right way which is why psychic readers follow this as a full-time occupation. This job can be done around the clock or at odd hours or fixed hours depending on the availability and urgency of both the reader and client.

In my previous sections, I mentioned psychic readers are people like many of you reading this. They have a spouse, children, their dreams and a lifestyle they live up to which definitely needs money to be taken care of smoothly. Just like everyone, they too pay taxes on their earnings. Thus, at a professional level, this is a wholesome job which needs utmost dedication and contribution to make it successful for both parties.

There are possibilities your psychic reader may not be immediately available due to personal reasons which mean family commitments or anything that has got to do with their own lives. They have their own homes to manage and just like you love spending time with your family, they do that too. They are no different from what you are, except the skills they possess.

Myth #8 – Psychics can see everything coming!

Psychics possess skills by developing an expertise in mediumship. Just like television, a medium's mind has an 'on' and 'off' switch. When a medium switches their psyche on they can read through each thought and feel every energy around them. Once they are done with reading, they come out of their psychic mode and turn off their psychic switches.

The point is that we have these energies around us all the time. We tend to not think about that because we do not put ourselves in a position where we would concentrate on feeling these powers. Even the most intuitive and powerful psychics do not gauge forthcomings unless they bring themselves together in the process of connecting with the outer world.

Change is inevitable which is why there is a high possibility that the readings may differ from actual happenings and that does not mean you are going to the wrong reader; everything that happens takes its own course to come into existence. Sometimes situations that are shared may not be immediate but could be something that may happen after a particular amount of time.

Myth #9 – Mediums are able to give answers or details of all questions asked

A lot of people feel that psychic readers can answer all the questions asked of them. Some of them even try to test them by asking them basic details of the past from their loved ones. Now, what happens with spirits is that they keep very selected memories of their past. For example, if your medium connects with a loved one you've had lots of memories with and just to test if you're with the right one you may ask them to share details of a specific happening. It's not necessary that your psychic reader may give you an answer for it, the reason being the one I stated above. There are possibilities that your loved one has erased that particular memory from their energy which is why your medium did not get an answer for that memory.

The process of getting information and facts through mediumship is supposed to be effortless. You have to trust in the energies and must accept that not all spirits carry details. Some can and will share whereas some spirits will just not be able to. The medium cannot force a spirit to give details that are not registered with them anymore.

Spirits answer details that are stored in them; some people conclude that a reader is not efficient enough if they do not get obvious answers to their questions. A psychic reader is a medium and only knows the information that is shared by your loved one based on the memories they kept within themselves.

Myth #10 – Mediums can get through to any and every spirit the client wants to connect with

This one is a commoner among people who want to connect with their loved ones. A good and honest medium will make it very clear that unless the spirit of your loved one wants he will not be able to connect with them. There are many reasons psychic readers are unable to connect with the spirit of your choice, such as your loved one may be undergoing the process of healing or may be involved in learning, training or may have any other reason.

You must understand that a medium cannot force a connection with spirits, it has to come naturally, and it's your loved one's choice if they would like to connect with you or not. There are possibilities a spirit is not willing to connect with a psychic reader; it could be any reason stated above or any other reason or circumstance that would not allow a medium to connect with them.

Myth #11 – Getting readings done from a psychic can open channels of positive and negative energies

Psychic readers who follow healthy practices attract high-quality spirits. A medium who is honest about their services will attract spirits with good energy; it is very similar to the Law of Attraction which is your energies, positive or negative, will attract similar other energies. Honest psychic readers develop a positivity in them which helps them connect with you at a deeper level where you will feel safe and secure.

High-quality psychic readers lure good spirits that do not harm you and have no negative energies and adverse effects. Connecting with a loved one in the form of a spirit can make you sensitive towards sensations, but that has got nothing to do with the kind of energies it brings into your life. An honest psychic reader will never take advantage of the incorrect information you have collected over the years that have formed into a myth. They will always be very clear about how things work when it comes to getting in touch with outside sources.

Myth #12 – Mediums can remove you from the spell of a curse or can curse you

A lot of superstitious people believe that a curse is a mishap that is sure to happen but in its true sense it is a wish that comes off a person's mouth in anger or resentment. A few psychic readers practicing unhealthy mediumship do take advantage of a person's misbeliefs and misguide them into malicious practices. You must understand a curse is a negative energy that enters in your life only if you allow it to, similar to the Law of Attraction.

There are a few instances where a person could be possessed and under the influence of negative energies. In such cases, it is a good medium's responsibility to help them out of such a circumstance and teach them how to keep such spirits away from them.

Myth #13 – There are fixed times when a loved one connects with you through a medium

In this chapter I have mentioned connections between a medium and spirits. If a spirit is comfortable with connecting with you, it will not take very long to do so. However, if they are experiencing healing or they are raising themselves up they may not immediately come to your rescue.

It is always advisable to be in your strongest and healthiest mental state when you book an appointment for your reading. Trust your intuition; it will tell you when you are ready to connect with your loved one.

Sometimes it does not take long to establish a connection with a loved one, whereas there are times when you may not quickly connect with them or may not be able to connect at all. The psychic reader is not responsible for not being able to build a bridge between the two of you but it's the spirit who holds the power to connect, re-establish or not connect with a medium or mediums at all.

Always remember a simple fact about psychic readers, anyone of them who is positive and honest will always show you the right path. A medium, if he or she follows positive energies and does their work honestly, will be clear with you from the very beginning, giving you the closure that you need regardless of whether they can get in touch with your loved one or not. If you ever come across a psychic reader who goes against the energies above and tries to misguide you, do not stay quiet, please go to a legitimate institute that would help you investigate the truth.

Like I keep saying, this is a process – a lengthy one or at least one that needs a lot of patience. Trust in your medium and do not feel overwhelmed when you are unable to get your answers or get in touch with the outer energies.

Chapter 4 – Honing your Mediumship and Psychic Abilities

Mediumship and psychic ability is something that you can hone. Also called channeling in the modern times, mediumship requires you, as the channeler, to work as the receptive agent or the channel for all forms of intelligent communications that come from the spiritual world. You may have a hard time accomplishing this at first, especially if you are still a beginner, but rest assured that with practice, you will eventually hone this ability

First and foremost, you need to know that possessing psychic abilities is not a special ability given only to a few by the Almighty. It is a skill, an expertise that is developed in order to help people bond with their loved ones. This skill can only progress if you keep yourself healthy in heart, in mind, and in body. The energies present in your body will help you be a quality psychic reader and will favor your connection with the right energies when you practice it. Meditation is one of the best methods to maintain your calmness and to develop concentration which is an absolute essential to successfully approach this form of psychic and mediumship.

This final chapter of this book will walk you through some tips that will help develop your mediumship and psychic abilities. After reading this book, you will be armed with more information about how you can perform the process of channeling and ensure that you decipher the message from those on the other side of the world accurately.

1. **Trust in yourself and your own abilities** – If you don't believe in yourself, then you will be blocking your chance of learning everything that you need to learn about mediumship. Note that negative thoughts have a tendency of hindering your psychic abilities. No matter how long it takes, stay upbeat and do not lose faith in your ability. You will eventually reach your goals.

You can also further develop your trust in your own abilities by finding inspiration from various sources. You can do so by reading success stories of those who were able to develop their psychic and mediumship skills. Aside from believing in yourself, you also need to trust your own power and the power of supernatural beings. Never doubt anything related to the spiritual world. Let go of any doubts before starting your spiritual ventures.

Unless you have confidence, nothing will work out, and this fact is applicable for not just mediumship but also any other aspect of life. You must know we all have the ability to gauge energies around us. Some of us turn into mediums while some do not pay much attention to this facet of nature. If your aim is to be a psychic reader, you must believe that you can, proceed with honing your skills, and comfort people with your abilities.

2. **Relax** – Make it a point to reach a deep relaxation state prior to starting your spiritual journey. You can do this through slow breathing and meditation while also concentrating on stillness and nothingness. Aside from clearing your mind, such relaxation techniques are also capable of changing your brainwave patterns, relieving tension and improving your metabolic rate.

    Relaxation through meditation and slow, yet deep breathing also works in temporarily altering your prefrontal cortex, thereby giving you the chance to boost your energy levels and mental performance. These are exactly what you need to stay in touch with the spirits. You need to release stress and breathe, so you can freely communicate with the spirits and accurately decode their message.

    The best ways to relax is to exercise or put your energy into something that makes you feel good. It could be helping people or undertaking a new activity or even listening to music. If you have a stressful life, try taking some time off and being alone so that you can spend time with yourself, thinking about the larger aspects of life.

3. **Be at peace with yourself and with those around you** – Remember that you will have a hard time unlocking your mystic gifts and channeling abilities if you don't resolve any conflicts and differences that you have with yourself and others. Let go of fights and resolve all forms of conflict in your life.

If arguments are inevitable, then try to argue in a constructive manner and work on achieving a final resolution. Hurting yourself and others due to your unresolved conflicts and unmanaged anger can prevent you from lifting the burden off your shoulders. You will have a hard time clearing your head, which is extremely important in your attempt to communicate with the spirits.

It is very important to be constructive at all times in your life. You have to be emotionally healthy to come to the point of neutrality where you do not negatively react to stressful and negative circumstances. The best way to improve your ability to connect with deep energies is that you must move consciously towards keeping yourself happy and relaxed by doing things that keep you happy. See the good in every situation around you; this takes time. Developing an ability where you can stay calm with all kinds of people who are happy, sad, angry or people possessing drastic or extreme characteristics, can help you build your skill as a medium.

4. **Get rid of your fear of the supernatural phenomena** – While it is frightening to deal with the supernatural phenomena at first, you should never allow your fear to hinder your chance of improving your mediumship and psychic abilities. Be open to getting in touch with your spiritual gift, instead of fearing the consequences. While it is possible that you will foresee some things at times when you don't expect them, instill in your mind that those are all part of the experience.

Embrace your gift because there is no reason for you to fear it.

Establishing a connection with a spirit can be scary especially when you have heard a million fallacious stories with no proper proof. The thing is, you have to be mentally prepared and assured that nothing will go wrong. A spirit can never harm you substantially because you are connecting them with people who are in need of them and who love them. So there are negligible chances that it would have any negative effect on you.

5. **Develop positivity** – Do what it takes to be contented with life. This may involve taking a break so you can spend some time with yourself from time to time or continue to do that hobby that you once found enjoyable. You need to showcase a more positive attitude.

   Learn what makes you smile and what you can do to let go of all forms of negativity and stress. Your positive attitude is crucial in your attempt to achieve spiritual freedom, thereby making it easier for you to hone your mediumship abilities. Eliminate all your worries so you can attain a deeper level of consciousness.

   In the world where there is an abundance of negative energy, it can be difficult to stay positive. The Law of Attraction is known to all, but there are very few who can practice it because they put in efforts to bring in the change. Look at the positive side of each situation. There is always a good thing shaping up when things are going wrong. After all, they say, there's light at the end of every dark tunnel.

6. **Develop your psychometry skills** – Psychometry is one of the most interesting ways to develop or improve your clairsentience, which is one means of obtaining intuitive information through feelings. Psychometrics has got a lot to do with understanding personalities, abilities, and attitudes. Once you develop your psychometry skills,

you can learn more about objects via touch, and that's possible just by reading the energy surrounding such objects.

Understanding someone helps you empathize and easily connect with them so as to be able to make them feel comfortable. This skill can help you put your client at ease who comes to seek help from you. Knowing how to deal with another being can make it easier for you to move forward in your attempt to gain knowledge in the field of mediumship.

One effective exercise that can help you hone your psychometry skill, which is also crucial in the field of mediumship and challenging, is to touch an object with an unknown history. Touch it until you obtain intense feelings about it. Try connecting to the past using it. Concentrate. Do you start to feel something about the past of the object or its owner? If you don't feel something yet, avoid forcing your vision or pressuring yourself.

Just continue touching it without any pressure. Avoid wallowing in despair and frustration just because you don't feel anything. Note that there are times when this will happen. The main reason is that not all objects have interesting stories.

7. **Improve your remote viewing skills** – Remote viewing refers to that psychic ability which allows you to mentally visit a place. This means that you don't have to go to that place physically. You can practice this skill by visualizing a place you plan to visit. You don't have to pick a fancy one. You can even choose to imagine your friend's house or the grocery store.

There could be instances that the person you are thinking about a lot on a particular day could be seen in your dreams doing something you want them to do. Your thoughts materialize through your dreams which is why you see places and people you subconsciously want to visit or have in your life.

Imagine being at a specific place before sleeping. You should then note the colors, objects, and people in your dream. Find out which among these things perfectly match the place when you get the chance to really go there. It is also advisable to write important details from your dream so you can retain them in your memory.

8. **Learn more about your spirit guides** – It is possible for you to get to know more about them through meditation. During each of your meditation sessions, it is advisable to ask your spirit guides if they can show themselves. Ask about their names. Avoid filtering anything. A wise tip to become a great medium is to go with the flow and learn to trust yourself.

   Deciding to meet with your spirit guides, as well as your entire spiritual team composed of teachers, angels, and masters is an interesting way of developing your mediumship abilities. Meeting your spirit guides is easier through meditation. What you have to do is to prepare yourself to meditate, but make sure that you set your intention prior to starting the session. Your intention should be your desire to know your spirit guides.

   In case they don't show up to introduce themselves, don't get frustrated. There are times when you need to spend more time developing trust and practicing the skill, so don't pressure yourself too much if you don't get it the first time.

   You also need to utilize your imagination when planning to know more about your spirit guides. Buy a journal and pen, so you can begin writing and allow your imagination to flow freely. Just make sure that you are in a quiet and relaxing place when writing. Use your imagination wisely, as well.

It is an effective means of opening up your mediumship and psychic abilities since it allows you to go out of your thinking mind. Once you are in this state, consider asking questions, like the names of your spirit guides, their appearance, their clothes, and personality. This will let you know them on a deeper level.

In this book, it is mentioned a couple of times that the approach of developing a mediumship skill can be very lengthy and could bring disappointment time and again regardless of how many years you've been in the practice of attracting energies. You have to be patient while pursuing advances related to mediumship.

9. **Develop clairvoyance through random and flower visualization** – Most visualization exercises are designed in such a way that these can help you hone your mediumship and psychic ability, more specifically, clairvoyance. Flower visualization works by grabbing flowers from a bouquet or from your own yard. It would be nice to use different kinds of flowers in this form of visualization. The flowers should be arranged in front of you. Study them.

   Once done, you can close your eyes. Visualize that you are one of the flowers arranged in front of you. Once you see a flower clearly using your mind with your eyes closed, you can move on to the next one until you have completed the exercise.

   Random visualization, on the other hand, is a fun exercise. What you have to do is to allow yourself to relax with your eyes closed. Put your focus on the area where the third eye is. The next step is to invite or ask your spirit guides to show peaceful and nice pictures to you. Avoid thinking. Just allow your mind to wander freely and let the pictures flood your third eye.

   Clairvoyance is not as difficult as the other stages of mediumship are. It can be practiced through visuals on your screen or any objects around you. Concentration is the key to developing this ability. Put all your energy and focus in the center and experience visuals you never thought existed.

10. **Heighten your vibration** – High vibration is crucial in honing your mediumship and psychic abilities. The main reason is that spirits are capable of vibrating at an extremely high frequency. With your high vibration, you can easily sense when the spirits are already around. It also allows you to live a more authentic and joyful life, making it easier for you to connect to the Divine, to your Higher Self, and to the spiritual realm. With your increased vibration, you will also get the chance to attract spiritually aware and beautiful souls. Practicing your psychic ability is easier that way.

    The best possible way of connecting with quality souls is by bringing positivity in to your vibrations. Eat, exercise, think and be healthy in all aspects of your life, and this is how you will allure spirits with high caliber. The positivity in your aura is how your client will feel the most secure and will be able to trust in you and your skills without a doubt. Great psychics are people who look towards energies that help them and others to receive knowledge and information that is not easily available on the surface of this earth. Utilize your skills to its maximum level to move forward with your endeavors.

Concentration plays a cardinal role in building your ability to be a bridge between a client and his or her loved one. Remember, when you were a young kid, and you wanted to ride a bike like a pro, what did you do? You kept practicing riding until you were confident enough to take off the side wheels and ride freely. Yes, it's the same logic that you would apply here; you've got to keep pursuing your skills until you feel assured of helping your client. Keep practicing and developing your attentiveness towards the energies around you and this is how you will be able to get develop a deeper sense of physic and mediumship.

Chapter 5 – Reasons for Mediumship

In the practice of channeling, it is mainly seen to be as the person's body being overcome by another spirit. Think of it as the body being taken through another world or another dimension as the soul is then able to communicate with other spirits. Once the body is there, it is able to ask questions and talk. After, the body returns to normal life and the soul has received the answers for the mind to hear. There are many stories that are able to tell what happens more in detail as many people face different effects of communication. These kind of stories are done through the work of shaman, prophets, witch doctors, and other people who have gone through their own daily routine to hear voices through the walls or through the air.

The main people used for the communication with spirits are called Channelers. These are the type of people who have been known to have a kind of psychic medium. They use 'spirit guides' to call upon friendly spirits to request their presence for the purpose of guidance and knowledge. Being able to channel is spirit involves unfolding the spirit of the body and the spirit of the outside. It is meant to transform the spirit to bring a new light to the person themselves. As the channel begins to develop with the friendly spirit, a bridge develops to the higher realms of the universe where the souls are thought to be found. Although this gives lots of power to the mind, it stills involves the constant action of shifting the mind through the mental space of dimensions in order to have the most open mind possible for outside spirits to find and enter.

To achieve this open mind, there were many things that can be practiced mentioned earlier in the previous chapters. With the constant time of relaxing and understanding the use of nature, the fields of mediumship meant for opening up the mind for communication are able to be strengthened. Basic meditation is one of the best ways to break yourself from the grip of reality and enter another place. It is seen as a place for relaxation and allowing the mind to rest, but for the purpose of communicating with outside spirits it is best to see meditation as the main way to open up the mind for communication. The Channelers are able to meditate in order to break away from the thoughts or influences of the world and then tune into the higher conscious where the body's soul is able to be found.

The reasons behind all of this goes on through many other books and many other places. People are curious and sometimes books are not enough. Sometimes the answers do not actually exist. Sometimes questions in life remain unanswered for a reason. When this happens, some people choose to go through the use of spirits to find their own answers. They find the right people to guide them, or they work by themselves in order to heal their own mind and soul.

• **Evidential Mediumship**

The first reason why people choose to go through the use of spiritual communication is for the use of evidential mediumship. They are able to use the answers of outside spirits to communicate with their own loved ones. If a person has experienced the death of a loved one, it can be rather tragic and painfully for many months or even years. This can leave an unsettling feeling where the person wishes to hear from them again or ask a question that they had been waiting to ask. Some people would see it as a sign of hope while other people would question the point of communicating with the souls of a loved one. They would even ask how they would know the spirit is truly the spirit of their own loved one or why the spirit would want to come back to the earth in order to simply communicate. How would the spirit get the needed answers and how much would they need to go through in order to get the answers. All of these questions keep bouncing around between different books and articles. The main point is how people use mediumship for communicating one more time with a loved one. Many questions come up with this concept, but every question does have an answer somewhere.

Seeking the communication of a past beloved spirit is used to help heal or answer a place of separation. Spirit communication is able to get through the pain of loss to bring together two people who became separated. It brings together a part of two people that used to exist but was lost through death. The pain of separation makes people think more about their loved ones and the connection of death. They want to communicate with their loved ones again to see if they are okay. They want to see if they were actually able to pass on to another place and see if they are in comfort. A loved one will continue to be a loved one even through death. Being able to communicate with the spirit of a loved one can ensure that they are alright and that they are able to continue on.

Knowing that a lost loved one is alright can help to ease the mind. Sometimes it comes with a follow up question of where they are. People continue to be curious and they continue to want answers. The action of mediumship is able to answer all of these kind of resounding questions. In past actions of spirit communication, it was mainly seen that when a person dies, the soul in not separated by distance, but by dimension. The only thing that is left behind in death is the physical body of the person and their possessions. While there is still grief and pain in the loss of a loved one, it can bring more comfort knowing that they still exist somewhere in the universe and that they are still able to be heard. Sometimes it only takes one voice and one more chance to heal the harshest wound.

People that have worked with mediumship to communicate with loved ones that proved many different cases of evidence. It has shown that hearing the person's voice or getting an answer from the loved one is a large area of healing, resolve, and closure. Just think, how many times after losing someone do you think about them? How many times do you make that one wish to hear from them once more? How many times were you willing to give up everything just to know that they are alright? In these times, thoughts are wandering and going so quickly that the person is not even able to think. Compared to thinking of them each and every day, how many times are they are to communicate with them spiritually? How often are people able to hear the voices of their loved ones?

Once they are able to successfully communicate, they are able to say or ask anything that they want to. They have a second chance to apologize for anything they did. They have a second chance to say how they truly feel about the other person, and probably the most important is being able to say 'I am sorry'. Whether something happened or not, it is natural to apologize for possibly not spending the right amount of time or thought on something. Other times, saying it can bring comfort simply as a safety of not feeling worried or concerned about being judged.

Probably one of the more interesting things about death is how it is able to change the paths of life. It may not be able to give the answers about what life is for or what life is about, but it can give another path to life. After losing someone, it can feel traumatizing and make the person feel lost. When communicating with the spirit of the loved one, it can help to get the answers to these kind of questions.

In a sense, death can be seen as a journey. Taking yourself from one world to another. Moving from one purpose to another purpose. Enjoying yourself in another dimension. Instead of thinking of loss, think of it as your loved has a second chance to live another great life. While it is sad to lose someone, it is best to think in a rather positive way when taking the next step through to mediumship. Sometimes, the medium of communication is willing to give more details such an addresses, names, and phone numbers. Not for where they are, but to help guide you to another opportunity. For example, if you are communicating with a lost loved one through mediumship, the spirit might wish to guide you through to another home or another workplace to help get you through the grieving process. Even after the death has taken place, there is still care and the thought or supporting each other. This is the main reason why people choose to communicate with their loved ones after death.

• Inspirational Mediumship

Every time a person decides to communicate through mediumship, they have the chance of a spirit coming forward to get them information towards life. For many years and even centuries, spirits have communicated to provide the wonders and mysteries of both life and death. Whether it is concerning the aspect of birth and bring a soul into the world, the aspect of creation with the world forming and growing each day, or the aspect of death to cause sorrow and grief, they provide answers. They want to help and show that they are real. In other cases, they have shown themselves to be cautious of the times ahead in the present moment and recommended changing certain actions that could be detrimental to the communicator's life. Even psychic researchers have seen these times come into the light as they pass through the different mediums of the universe and travel through the different times of triumphs.

One of the more current researchers on this type of subject is named Harry Price. In his times through different mediums of communication, he has been able to spot many differences in which they are able to catch themselves to see who these spirits are. He has mentioned before that the mental mediums of spirits normally are women who do not have any kind of qualities to themselves. They are neither intellectual nor physiological. While they were easily distinguished away from the other males, they still appear as if they are from a somewhat educated part of society. Even though they do not have any kind of true qualities, they put on an act to express themselves to the communicator. These kind of occurrences with the female spirits are normally rather puerile. They will appear rather stale with the religious uplift of their own previous mind.

Even after all of this has been seen from the spirits, this researcher himself has been able to view them in a different form of evidence. He has questioned if the evidence is actually real. While some of the spirits might be able to prove themselves to be the loved one of the person communicating, who is to say that they are saying the right communication? While this has gone on for over one hundred years of people and researchers continuing to be skeptical, he still goes on to show the reality of communicating and how it should be taken more lightly than people think. This is not to ridicule anyone and it is not to show a bad cause towards other people who are trying mediumship. This researcher is simply saying to be careful.

With hearing a message and not knowing how to interpret it, Harry Price has told people to take the words from the spirit as a kind of inspiration for themselves to have. It takes a fair amount of energy for the mind to handle to cross all the different boundaries found in the center of the mediums. A person who was successfully able to get through to hear the voice of a spirit should be proud and take in the words of the spirit with caution. Since this researcher continued through to question many of the dead relatives of people and questioned the reality of the mediumship people go through, he himself is questioned for the purposes of inspirational mediumship.

This researcher goes on to explain more about the inspiration given to people by the spirits, but never truly goes on to continue with the reasons behind the inspiration. He never continues to think about how people should work within themselves to find the balance of mediumship for people to follow. He never answers or questions the reasons on why the spirit would give these moments of inspiration to the people who are communicating. It is more than simply giving them a reason or path of life, it is about opening up the mind.

When the spirit says an action that should be done, it is best to think of it as a suggestion rather than a demand. On one side, the action could be good and change the life of the person communicating in a very positive way. On the other side, the action could be bad and cause more pain in the future or present moments of your life. When the spirit talks about the world and how it is changing, it is best to think of it as a warning or subtext to the main point. If they are talking about the lands breaking apart, it could be either about the society that lives on the land or it could be about the actual land itself breaking apart by an earthquake. The spirit is not necessarily trying to trick you, they are simply trying to get a message through to give a direction to follow. The choice to follow the path mentally or physically is yours.

Just as evidential communication was about bringing two separate mediums or dimensions to one place, inspirational mediumship does the same. It is the kind of communication that exists naturally within every person. It is a type of wonder that is found deep within our souls and gives each person's mind to pass through the dimensions of communication. Many things in the world have been given to society to adore. From inspiring lectures to stunning paintings to advances in technology, the world has gone through many changes through the generations. Sometimes people might not agree with communicating with the spiritual life since it can cause a burden to life, but other people continue to see inspiration from it.

With the idea that the spirit grows within a person's soul and that they will continue on through life to go beyond wonders, answers can be found from this idea. Some cases of mediumship have suggested that people created the wonders of the world today from their own kind of intellectual knowledge and creativity. As more communication goes through with research, people have seen a connection between the soul and the creations found today in both science and art. Since many generations have past, there are many spirits that exist. One of the most interesting ideas from spirits in how they always look to inspire the spirits within other people. The spirit from outside every person's body continues to search for more ways to inspire the spirits within the person's body. No more what relationship the two different kinds of spirits had, they still continue this type of work. Being able to channel through and find the aspects of mediumship means that they are able to continue through to have this circle of inspiration exist within the boundaries of society.

The question that comes to many people, even the researchers, is what if the information given by the spirits is not meant to be inspiring? What if the information being given is only about wonder and never fact? If there are supposed to be many spirits that look to inspire, then why do some levels of disagreements exist during the communication? All of these kind of questions do lead people to question if this type of communication with spirits is even real. The first thing to keep in mind when these questions come up is how any communication with spirits has to go through the consciousness of the person communicating themselves. Since the spirit has to work to go through the thoughts of the mind, then it is more likely to be inspiring since they had to find their way there. The words of the spirit will then be inspirational to the spirit's mind or other kinds of personal attributes in the soul. The second thing to keep in mind is how not every spirit that a person comes across will view life the same way. There are many disagreements that force the same issues to come across the mind and the spirit. These issues are about how the earth should grow, how people should behave, and how society should belong. Important issues such as these come with many different opinions and answers that cause tension between the consciousness of the person and the spirit on the other side.

The one major difference between a person and a spirit is how much they are bound to the views on earth. In the world where people speak left and right about ideas, there exists a type of truth. In the spirit realms where creation began, there is only one way of communication where there exists an Ultimate Truth. God's truth. This truth is the truth that began the creation of the universe and all the lives that are around us. When a spirit is formed, deep with it exists this ultimate truth that humans are not able to truly grasp on their own. With the communication being more inspiring rather than detrimental, the deeper levels of the spirit have been found and heard. It is the voice of reason and the voice of God's truth that comes through the communication of the spirit.

The ideas of inspirational mediumship seek to have this kind of message for people to have. It looks to provide a sense of the truth in the spirit that can be used for other people to use for the rest of their lives. While there are many questions that a person is able to ask a spirit, they still have to see the ideas of the other side through answers. They must have an open mind and they must be willing to listen. Inspiration comes in many forms, and they all are found by people. All a person needs to do is stay calm and listen for the next opportunity to come before them.

• **Physical Mediumship**

Physical mediumship is the type of communication in which a spirit will work through the mental and physical energies of the medium and force a physical action to happen on earth. This kind of mediumship is the most profound and amazing demonstration of the outside spirits that surround people. While it is also the most mistrusted, it is also the highest form to interaction between the person and the spirit themselves. Since this process has started in the spirits, people have been able to recognize when it is actually happening around them. Whenever an object is knocked over or a random voice is heard, it is the spirit attempting to communicate with the person through a kind of physical form.

When in a state of deep trance, the spirit is able to sense the kind of energy a person has. If a person is known to be more vital, they will most likely have a kind of magnetic and etheric energy. This type of energy can be fed upon by the spirit themselves and it can then be manipulated in different forms. Whether the spirit uses the energy for travel or uses it for their own knowledge, the energy is able to be condensed and directed through the thoughts of the mind in order to go through to the spirit. Even though this is able to be done, the main source of energy for the spirits comes from the medium that they originate from. The main vital energy that the spirits need to order to have this kind of physical phenomena happen comes from the medium. Otherwise it causes the person to lose energy. If there is an abundance of energy in a room for a spirit to gain, then the physical phenomenons are meant to be stronger.

Once the spirit enters the room, they are given the option to be in control of the medium. Through a trance, the physical phenomena is able to start. From there, the mind of the person communicating is in control of the energies in the room and is then able to manipulate them. Whether the energy is used to speak with the spirit or not, it is able to be manipulated through the mind. This is able to be done through the ectoplasm of the person. This is able to create a limitless amount of physical phenomena to happen around them. The ectoplasm is the material that is from the body within the room being controlled. It is the etheric matter that is known to be invisible and easily subjected to forms of mental influences. Whatever makes a person who they are and whatever makes them capable to controlling a physical medium is found within the ectoplasm. Sometimes it is very dense and strong so that the person is easily able to communicate with outside spirits. Other times it is more about how much they are able to wait since they do not have as much of the ectoplasm material within themselves.

A person named Nandor Fodor wrote about this idea in his book 'Encyclopedia of Psychic Science'. In it, he describes the ectoplasm as a more mysterious material for the human mind to consider. He goes through to explain how much it is a substance of manipulation that continually streams out of the body and causes forms of intelligence to form. To him, it is a phenomena of physical order that includes both sides of partial and complete materialization. From Professor Richet, he discovered that the first thing established in the spirit of a person is their own ectoplasm matter. This matter according to the professor is invisible and intangible in its own primary state of being a liquid. As it goes through the stages of condensation, it is able to be utilized through the spirits and manipulated for the purposes of communication. In this case, physical mediumship through the spirit compounding this ectoplasm matter.

With everything a spirit can do as it is able to travel through different bodies and mediums, it brings up the question of why they would want to go through the energy of physical phenomena. What kind of purpose does it show for both the person and the spirit themselves? The answer is actually quite simple. Through the use of physical objects, the spirit is able to make themselves known for the purpose of communication. Sometimes, people are harder to get to and they sometimes refuse the presence of a spirit. If they are able to see a physical message from the spirit in front of them, then they will be more likely to carry through with the process of communication. The sight of physical mediumship by the spirit is more profound than the other kinds of mediumship. Anything that happens physically by the spirit can easily be transcribed by the human mind. It is able to show the power of the human mind and it is able to show the impact on human matter by a spirit. Whether the table moves or a glass falls over, it is the spirit trying to show you a different way of communication to follow.

Chapter 6 – Developing Mediumship

With all the reasons to communicate with a spirit, many people have the urge to continue and try it out for themselves. Whether they are truly all by themselves or seek the help of a professional, being able to speak with a spirit will be able to give insight on what path to take if a person is lost in life. If they are not sure what to do, sad about the death of a loved one, or simply wanted a few questions answer, reaching out for help is not a bad thing. A spirit is able to guide a person onto the right path.

Being able to develop the aspects of mediumship within yourself involves lots of time, hard work, patience, and the dedication of studies. Even though people in books and on television will show the process being instant, there is nothing instant that happens when starting to communicate. If you are looking to start communicating through mediumship, it is best to start with the steps below.

The first thing to do is find a group of people who share the same interest. If you are able to find people with the same interests as you outside of communicating through mediumship, then this step will be easier. If not, there is no need to worry. Mediumship by itself is always developed in a circle. This circle is quite literally referred to as the 'development' or 'spirit' circle. The development circle that is created should include only people who are looking to communicate with spirits. Not only that, but the circle should include a person who knows basically what they are doing. This leader should be able to understand the energy of the room and the mediumship unfoldment or development. The rest of the people should remain calm. In this circle, the aiming point is to have about seven or eight people. While the amount of people does not matter, this size has been shown to be one of the better sizes for this event of communication.

The second thing to do is to determine the kind of mediumship that you might want to work on. Be ready to share it with the group of people in the circle since only one kind of mediumship should be worked on at a time. It is not advisable to have more than one mediumship worked on at a time. The circle of people should be willing to either work on the development of physical mediumship or mental mediumship. Both of these will require a rather general format to work through and a very specific energy to be formed in the room.

The third thing to do is work on a schedule. Once a group has been found and brought together, they are then needed to count upon each other. Because of this, it is important for each member of the group to be willing to meet at a specific time. Whether it is once a week or twice a week, it is best to meet every time at a specific time on these days. Once a spirit has been contacted and is able to go through to get into the energy of the room, then the spirit will link itself to the same schedule. That way the group will be able to have a better time communicating with the spirit themselves. As for the circle itself, people should not only show up on time but they should also sit in a certain seating arrangement. During the first meeting, the seating arrangement should be set and possibly written down to make sure that no one is out of place. The assigned seats for each person should not change unless the leader of the group sees that a shift in the energy of the room is necessary. In time, other people are allowed to enter the group and join the circle. This can be seen when the energy of the room and the spirit together is fully balanced. From there, the seating arrangement would change and then the energy of the room can be worked with. Having a new person entering the circle starts the process again with the spirit and strengthens the energy of the room.

The fourth thing to do is figure out a preferred circle format. The leader inside of the circle should find the best format to use when calling the energy together in the room and then calling upon the spirit. No matter what the circle needs or who is in the circle, the first thing to always be done is an opening prayer. This prayer will call to God and Spirit for communication and protection. The second thing to do is a guided meditation practice. A meditation to help stimulate the sensitivity inside of each person in the circle. The third thing to do in the circle is message work. This message work is when the people inside of the circle will write to the spirit or work with the spirit to answer any questions written in the message. The final thing to do is a closing prayer as a group. With every circle or group comes a different practice and then a different leader. Some leaders choose to put the messages to the spirit before the meditation. Both formats will give success. Both will require strength and patience within each person to give them all an opportunity in a balance of energy with the spirit. Remember to keep the meditation exercises challenging each time. The purpose of the circle is to give development towards the limitation of each person. Having a constant energy in each person will only work for a temporary amount of time. Once they are able to complete meditations as normal, the energy will not be able to increase. But, if each person is challenged then they are able to have higher energy for the next meeting.

The fifth thing to do is work out the amount of time that should be spent in the circle during each meeting. The circle meeting for mediumship should not last longer than seventy five minutes, but they should still last at least an hour. When the circle meeting has ended, then they should work to keep the energy balanced in the room as they leave. In order to do this, everyone should stand up while in the circle when the meeting has ended. They should all then leave the circle area to dissipate the energy that was all formed during that same meeting.

The sixth thing to do is have patience. Being able to communicate with a spirit through mediumship takes lots of time and energy through each person. Mediumship is known to be one of the most beautiful things found within the connection of the spirit. It is like a pearl. It takes time and effort to grow. It does not grow overnight; instead it takes time and shows it beauty at the end. Once it is there, the beauty stays. Once the spirit is gathered and found, it can return. But getting to this point will take time. Remember to continue working hard in the group, studying hard in the methods, and being patient. Going through these steps will provide results as more time passes by. Working in the group of mediumship means working with the spirit. It is a group effort entirely. The spirit is tied to God, and He is the ultimate guide. This fact is the fact needed for success in the group.

Since the meetings are around an hour long, people should remember to arrive about ten or fifteen minutes before the circle is scheduled to begin. This will allow for people to take a breath and relax for a few moments. Being able to talk with each member of the group will resolve the cracks found in the mediumship. Having the care of each other and talk about the solutions to each worry of the day will give a positive energy to the group itself. But, there should be lines draw towards how much should happen between the group members in communicating. For example, do not offer drinks or refreshments. This will allow for more conversation to have or it will cause more caffeine to be within people. Any form of caffeine can cause a stimulant within the person and have it interfere with the work in the group that day. These refreshments may happen after the circle has met and attempted or succeeded when communicating with the spirit. Therefore energy has a possibility of staying balanced and a strong group connection can be formed.

After the circle meeting has completed and everyone has stepped out, the people in the group should discuss mediumship overall and what they learned in the circle. Under no kinds of circumstances should the people in the group talk about the messages of the spirit. This will foster the dialogue of the conversation and give out information that could mess up the messages of the next meeting. The main rule most leaders lay down from the first meeting is that there should be no more messages once the circle is closed. The last thing to do is figure out a study guide that will guide the members of the group. In order to find the best study guide for people to follow, it is best to find the kinds of trance and channeling for the group to have.

Trance and Channeling

In the recent studies and years of mediumship, areas of channeling have been rather misunderstood. Many people in this field will call them 'trance' channels. To start the understanding of what should really be done, start with the spirit. The spirit begins by linking itself to the medium of the room. The communications of the spirit will exert different levels of control with the energy found in the medium.

A trance is still considered to be one of the strongest degrees of control a person can have. There are different levels and different degrees of a trance from very light trances to very deep trances. The deep kind of trances are the ones that are mainly used for the physical mediumship. There are many different factors that affect the factors of control in a trance. Many different people who have studied to become parapsychologists have shown that different people have different levels of control within energy. A genuine trance has a sense of a strong connection with both mental and physical energies between the consciousness and the spirit themselves. Normally, when people start to enter a trance, they will begin to have a certain set of reactions. This can include a slower heart rate, a slower or deep breathing, no rapid eye movement, a lower body temperature, a highly reduced reaction to pain or touch, and then various moments of unconsciousness. Since a trance is where the spirit is able to speak directly to the person, then they go through the medium and restore the energy of the person as they continue to be in the trance.

From this trance, the spirit will be able to give a voice of reason for the person themselves to recognize. To get to this point, it is best to start by sitting. Taking away the mind from reality by calming the muscles. The next step is to go through and breadth. Close your eyes and open up your mind. Begin then by thinking about the energy of the room. Feel the environment around you slowly moving away as you enter a place of certainty. A place of connections. A place where a spirit can be found. Continue to do this with the guidance of a leader in mediumship.

An important thing to consider is how research in this area has shown that there are different areas of language dialogue that exists within the barriers of communication in a trance. Most of the time, there is a broken speech pattern that might have either a reversed sentence structure or a broken speech pattern. To solve this, it is best to read through previous cases of evidence in other books. It is best to talk to the leader in the circle or talk to a normal leader in mediumship. The second important thing to remember is how control works within a trance. Knowing what it means to be controlled by a spirit. The first thing to realize is how the medium or room the person is in is not possessed personally by the spirit themselves. Have a room or person possessed is rare. There is more of a share between the mental and physical energies between the spirit and the person. The control the spirit has in this communication will show a kind of telepathic introduction for the person. The control can be for either inspired thoughts that the person should hear, or it can be for a message to appear. Whether it is in a deep or light trance, both sides will go through the levels of the spirit in order to get the answer they were asking for.

Chapter 7 – Consulting a Medium

Mediums and people who are psychics are not machines who can randomly gather a spirit. They are not able to go through and turn their skills on or off. There are many factors that come into play when it comes to channeling through to find different areas of communication with spirits. In one meeting, everything might be able to fall into place with finding the right person, the right spirit, and the right message. At other times, things could change. Every time a meeting happens with a medium, things have the change to either right or wrong. The best thing to do is figure out the best person to talk to with the most amount of evidence behind their belt.

To start, remember that the first meeting will not say everything about the medium. As it is shown that things can change and that anything can happen, the first meeting should not be completely judged. The failure to find, establish, or even maintain a connection with a spirit has nothing to do with the medium themselves. It is not the idea that they might have had a bad day, sometimes things are just not prepared enough and it is no one's fault. Sometimes the energy in the room might not be balanced enough to call upon a direct spirit. At other times, a spirit might just not be found. Either way, it is best to remember to have an open mind and give a second chance to the medium. Then the question becomes, how do you find the psychic medium that is needed for you?

The first thing to do to find the psychic medium is to know yourself basically. Be able to see if you are ready to go into this next level of communication. It is a higher level to reach that is hard to grasp since it either happens or it doesn't. Once it happens, there is no escape from the communication at that moment. This fact alone can bring up a lot of questions that can give a fair number stress to a person. Whether you choose to do it or not, remember that it is completely your choice. Once you are comfortable with the idea happening to you, then you can choose the person you want to work with. From there, you must choose between having a psychic or a medium. Both of these kinds of people will work on different levels and will offer a different amount or idea within the communication itself. A medium will go more so towards the direct communication with the spirit to find answers to the questions you are asking. A psychic will instead sit down and tune into your own energy levels and interpret them as the answers that you are looking for. A psychic sees that the answers are found in a person's energy while a medium sees that the answers are found within outside spirits.

The second thing to notice is what they are saying to you in order to get you to say yes to their services. If one of them promises you the world, then be careful about choosing them. Next, look at the amount of money that they are charging you. If it is an unreasonable high fee, then it can be pretty easily assumed they are only looking for money rather than payment for their own experience. If the service is god, it will reflect in the price of course. The service of a good medium or a psychic is truly invaluable. Expect to pay a reasonable amount of money, but remember to compare cautiously. There is a different between a fair price for services and an overpriced service.

Also, when it comes to what they say to you, be careful if they promise communication with a deceased loved one. While it has been done before in previous cases, no one can actually promise for this to happen. There is no guarantee that a person will be able to contact the spirit of their loved one. If the conditions are right and the medium you have chosen is suitable for the connection of communication with the loved one, then you will most likely get what you asked for. None of this can be determined even after the right medium is found. In general, just be cautious of who you are looking to find. Be careful of choosing the people who charge for every question or communicator. It should be one flat rate for a meeting. Not an adjustable fee for more questions. If they charge for every question, then you might have to pay more than you realized up front.

The third thing to do is understand the medium. In order to do this, first take out the idea of predicting the next meeting. While days in the future can be planned out, they cannot be set in stone. Nothing in the future is set in stone because the future has not happened yet. The second thing to do is understand why the spirit of a lost loved one would wish to communicate through a medium. Is it for career, finance, or another lifelong opportunity? The answer is no. The spirit is not there to tell us where to go to get the shortcuts. Instead, they are communicating simply to say that they are okay. To tell the people that they have passed on and that there truly is life after death. After that happens, then the spirit will work to inspire the person. To guide them through the troubles they are facing rather than give them a list of all the things they need to do to succeed. The spirit does not come to live the lives that we all have. It does not come through the areas of communication to force someone to live a certain way. The same idea here applies to psychics as well. Be sure to watch what you ask and what you say. It is never a good idea to turn the responsibility of your own to another.

The fourth thing to realize when choosing a medium is if they ask personal questions. Whether it is before or during the sitting meeting, they should not ask for any kind of personal information. Most of the time psychics or mediums will hunt for information that a person is hiding. They will continue asking until they get an answer. Once they get an answer, that same answer is returned through so called answer or response of a spirit. It could be part of a medium giving the answer to what a spirit said or part of a psychic reading. Either way, they can twist personal information to make it sound good to the client and get more money from them. No medium nor psychic needs to know anything about you. The only thing that they will need to know is your name. If they ask for any other information, do not offer it. There is no need to provide a date of birth or anything about your own past life. That is your own privacy that will not affect the process of communicating with the spirit. The only question that a medium should ask during a meeting is if you were able to understand a piece of information given to you. Only answer with a yes or a no. Do not give out any other details.

The fifth thing to realize is that this is your decision and therefore your time. You chose for this to happen to get answers. If a psychic or medium says that you are not able to record anything during the meeting, then leave that person. It is best to go through and think about how the time should be spent. Instead of thinking through the questions and panicking on whether or not you will remember anything, the best thing to do is stay calm. It is your time and your choice.

The last thing to remember is how the psychic phone lines work. The best way to describe these phone lines is that they do not work. They are simply there to make a quick sum of money from people who are too desperate. In the United States, these type of phone lines are actually becoming more of a thing in the past rather than a goal for the future. They seemed to be there to help, but for hundreds of dollars each hour being spent, no true psychic is at the other end. A true medium or psychic will respect the client and remember how money works. If they are true, then they will be able to give the best results at a fair price.

Steps to Building a Connection with a Spirit

In the exploration of mediumship, there are many different resources and many different sites that will give answers. However these answers will not all be the same. One answer will not be the same as the other. When it comes to connecting to a spirit, it does bring lots of excitement to people. It brings a new sense of wonder and creativity that has never been seen by many people. Because of this, there are many resources and book that are available online to purchase for study guides and other forms of help to find support in your own journey through spirit communication.

Being able to successfully communicate with a spirit can be a rather exciting and overwhelming process at the same time. It is the idea of the paranormal happening around us that gets to people's heads. For some people, the interest in starting to communicate with spirits comes from an experience that they faced. Whether they saw a ghost or felt a different kind of presence around them, the experience was enough to get them to go to the paranormal insight. For other people, it is more about the study of life and death. They go through to see how much comes with life and how much life comes after death. These people sometimes go on this path after they have faced the loss of a loved one and they want to go through and figure out what happens after a person dies. Being able to find the right resources to get the right first step can be quite overwhelming with all the resources available to people. Below are five steps that might be able to guide you onto the right path. These steps should be able to help you through the times of finding a medium and searching for the answers you need.

Step #1 - Searching

The first step is to allow the search to happen. Just like with anything else in life, it is best to relax and not get tense in order to have the best outcome possible in the event. When searching online to find the answers to what happens after death, they go through to seek comfort within themselves. Looking for answers is a way to grief a loss. It is not necessarily about talking to the dead, it is more about finding a new way to find a balance of comfort during a rather tragic time.

When someone has lost another, then one of the first things that goes through their mind is death. They question what death actually is and they try to understand the aspects of it. To start, look at cases of afterlife. Cases where people temporarily were dead and then came back. These are the people who have seen the other side and have then come back to life. While it is hard to hear about people coming back after experiencing the loss of another, think about these cases as a way of evidence. These people saw for themselves that something else does exist out there. They go through to guide people through videos and articles to show others what they saw. The second thing to do is find all the cases of real mediumship. Since there is lots of research that surrounds the areas of mediumship and communicating with spirits, there is evidence to show people how it works and why it is a good point to turn to. It is the fact that normal people who have lived an ordinary life have gone through to see, hear, and sense the presence of another outside spirit. It shows that something else is out there.

As mediumship research continues through the mental and physical experiences, more can be said on what is to happen. As the spirits of the outside are working to establish more of an outside connection, there brings up the idea of philosophy and religion. The ideas in life have the possibility of changing perspective the moment that a spirit enters and has a physical experience. It is not necessarily about seeing a full figure of a person. Instead it is more about watching something knock over or having a door open all the way by itself. In these situations, it is the spirit trying to show that they are there around you. Other times it is about how the spirit does not want to have you there. This is why it is best to research the possibilities and other cases of evidence that happened to other people.

When this happens to people when they see a paranormal experience happen around them, then it is best to find an expert for guidance. The people who explore these kind of ideas are called 'seekers'. These are the people who have spent many days and many months exploring the ideas behind the meaning of life, the different kinds of metaphysical perspectives, and other ideas outside of normal reality. They are looking for an understanding of the world as they work to relax and open up their mind to new ideas, people, and experiences.

Allowing the search is the very beginning of the journey. It is what allows a person's mind to travel through itself where more thoughts can be collected and more ideas can be understood. No matter how many books a person goes through or how many experts a person talks to, there is always something else out there. The areas of mediumship and speaking to spirits is a growing field that always gathers new cases of evidence. Being able to take the first step in searching online for what this communication is the most important start to remember. It is the first step that allows for a journey to other mediums and spirits around you.

Step #2 - Embracing the Sense

Once you feel comfortable and have begun the search to find the areas of mediumship, the next step is to find your own intuitive sense. Allowing this sense to open up will make it easier to communicate through with different spirits. It will begin to open up your own levels of awareness around you through books, websites, and the people supporting or guiding you through the journey.

This type of sense can come in many different forms, but there are three main forms that are normally seen with mediumship and spirit communication. The first one is called 'clairvoyance', the ability to clearly see. The second one is called 'clairaudience', the ability to clearly hear. The third one is called 'clairsentience', the ability to clearly feel. Once a person is able to take the first step forward, they are able to open up their minds to these senses. It is about declaring to yourself, your loved ones, your friends, your family, anyone you have lost, and the universe itself that you are ready to begin a sixth sense. Some people are born with this sense and pick it up quickly. Other people have to develop this ability naturally as they go through many cases of research and many other areas of discovery.

The most important thing to consider is how to embrace yourself to get the sixth sense. Once you are able to begin embracing the sixth sense in life, then you are able to begin seeing the true essence of the soul. This is the part that involves going through to see what is beyond your own physical body. What is past the heart and what exists inside of the soul. This new sense can be scary to grasp as it is different from the five other senses. It is not straight forward, it takes time and concentration to develop as your mind wraps around the idea of going beyond itself to reach a new limit. While reaching this level, remember that you still the one that is in complete control. You are in control of how fast or slow the process is. It does take time. You must continue to relax through the process and know that you are embracing the process. Be ready to sit down, close your eyes, and free your mind. The more you do this, the closer you will be to feeling everything around you. The air will feel different and time will not exist as you step closer and closer to this sixth sense.

Step #3 - Finding a Mentor

In Japan, they have teachers and clergy that are referred to as 'sensei'. They are the leaders who guide students along their own spiritual path of knowledge. In developing mediumship within yourself, it is important to find a sensei or a mentor. These are the people who have studied the ways of spirits for many years as they go through to provide a strong foundation for people to live upon.

Finding a mentor means that you will be able to have someone who can guide you. From there, you will be able to study under someone who is able to help you through the challenges and questions of mediumship. Building a connection to a spirit brings many different paths with all the research and information that is available. Having a mentor will be able to show you a single path rather than multiple paths. They will be able to push beyond the limits of your mind in order to open up your thoughts to the spirits. They know how to work through the levels of communication with spirits and they know how to find the best mind for it. All of this involves time and training. A training that involves working with the mentor to study and experience the sixth sense for mediumship.

There are people that might live in a smaller area who do not have access to these kind of mentors. They might be stuck, but only if they think that they are stuck. If the student is truly ready for this journey into mediumship, then the teacher will appear. Whether it is online through a support group, a book, a workshop, a movie, or a phone call, the teacher will appear once the student is ready.

Step #4 - Build your Support

While going through to study mediumship and reading through all the resources, it can become quite exhausting. The experience can become questioned for if it is really worth it. If you are working on your own through this journey, it is easy to get to these type of questions, otherwise it is best to strengthen yourself through a strong and solid support system. Mediumship is a very exciting process to go through, but going through it alone can prove to be too much on the mind. It is best to reach out to other people to find more areas of research and evidence in the outside world.

Some people choose to have their support system be their family or friends. Other people might not be able to have this type of support. They have to go through to find the best people another way. Since communicating with spirits can be a rather hard topic for people to grasp, it truly is hard to find the right people who would be willing to go with you through the journey. No matter what people say, it is best to remember that spirit communication can come from a place of love. A place of love that only God is able to come to. The whole universe is where spirits can be found, and He created it through love. As people continue to communicate with spirits, they are not looking to persuade or manipulate another person. Instead they are trying to strengthen an internal bond within themselves.

If this message still has not been able to provide a support group for you to follow, then don't lose hope. Continue going through the process of searching for the right people. Just like how it takes times to find mediumship, it might take time to find the best support group. Some church groups actually can be supportive of these actions. It is all about finding the best community that is able to share in the same ideas. All you have to do is keep trying and keep getting back up. If you really want to see the end of this journey, then you have to keep going to keep trying.

Step #5 - Recognize the Sacred

The last thing to do when building a connection with the spirit is realizing what it actually is. This doesn't mean accepting the idea for what it is or going through evidence to see what is out there in the world. Realizing the connection with the spirit means having an understanding of the spirit. Knowing that the connections that are created are all sacred within themselves. The thought of being a type of bridge that is able to connect one world to the next can be seen as quite a blessing. Being this bridge can be a service to others once the journey is complete.

The connection between the soul and the spirit within mediumship is strong enough to get through the moments of grief and other's times of tragedy. Once a communication has begun, you are then in the service of those others in spirit who have gone through to find you.

To truly recognize the sacred communication in the spirit, think about daily life. It is best to think about what aspects of your own life are seen as sacred as well. Whether it is a relationship with a person or a bond with an object, think about what it very valuable to you. Recognize the day to day connections around you and what makes these connections so special. Once you are able to see that the ability to communicate is the one thing that begins in the people around you, then you are able to see an opportunity in which both heaven and earth experiences are able to come together.

Most of the time after losing a loved one, people think continuously on what is would be like to see them again. They think about what it would be like to hear from them again. That type of connection is a sacred one for people to see. It is a connection in which the love was never lost. Even after death parts people, the love still exists through the pain of grief. This sacred connection can then be found when communicating with spirits. It is the type of connection that follows an awakening soul to find another spirit through mediumship.

Conclusion

Thank you again for downloading this book!

I hope this book was able to help you gather more information about mediumship, what it is, what it can do for you and its different types. This book has also provided you with some myths about mediumship, and the actual truths behind them. In the last chapter, you learned 10 powerful tips that will help hone your mediumship and psychic abilities. Now it is time to implement those tips.

Tap into your psychic power and be the best medium that you can ever be by applying the tips and knowledge that you have acquired in this book. Just make sure that you use your mediumship and psychic ability not for your personal gains, but to help yourself and others. Mediumship is a gift, so you have to use it to connect with spirits and non-physical beings without causing harm to anyone around you.

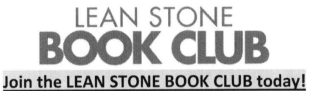

42482530R00040

Made in the USA
Middletown, DE
12 April 2017